# Let's Cooperate

By JONATHAN PEALE

Illustrated by TOM HEARD

Music Arranged and Produced by MUSICAL YOUTH PRODUCTIONS

## CANTATA
### LEARNING

WWW.CANTATALEARNING.COM

# CANTATA
# LEARNING

Published by Cantata Learning
1710 Roe Crest Drive
North Mankato, MN 56003
www.cantatalearning.com

**A note to educators and librarians from the publisher: Cantata Learning has provided the following data to assist in book processing and suggested use of Cantata Learning product.**

*Publisher's Cataloging-in-Publication Data*
*Prepared by Librarian Consultant: Ann-Marie Begnaud*
Library of Congress Control Number: 2015958184
    Let's Cooperate
    Series: School Time Songs
    By Jonathan Peale
    Illustrated by Tom Heard
    Summary: A song that teaches students how to cooperate with each other.
    ISBN: 978-1-63290-626-7 (library binding/CD)
    ISBN: 978-1-63290-635-9 (paperback/CD)
Suggested Dewey and Subject Headings:
    Dewey: E 395.5
    LCSH Subject Headings: Courtesy – Juvenile literature. | Students – Juvenile literature. | Courtesy – Songs and music – Texts. | Students – Songs and music – Texts. | Courtesy – Juvenile sound recordings. | Students – Juvenile sound recordings.
    Sears Subject Headings: Helping behavior. | Courtesy. | Students. | School songbooks. | Children's songs. | Popular music.
    BISAC Subject Headings: JUVENILE NONFICTION / School & Education. | JUVENILE NONFICTION / Music / Songbooks. | JUVENILE NONFICTION / Social Topics / Values & Values.

Book design and art direction, Tim Palin Creative
Editorial direction, Flat Sole Studio
Music direction, Elizabeth Draper
Music arranged and produced by Musical Youth Productions

Printed in the United States of America in North Mankato, Minnesota.
072016         0335CGF16

"Cooperate" is a big word! It means to do things together. How do we cooperate? We respect the people we work with. We listen to each other's ideas and help one another. Cooperating makes solving problems easier.

To see how you can cooperate with your classmates, turn the page and sing along!

5

Cooperate!

Cooperate!

When we all work together, it's great.

It's great!

It's a long, long word, but it must be heard. Let's co-op-er-ate!

Cooperate

When I play a game
and it's more than just me,
we all have fun
when it's two or three.

8

Here at school,

we play by the rules.

We cooperate!

Cooperate!

Cooperate!

When we all work together, it's great.

It's great!

It's a long, long word,
but it must be heard.
Let's co-op-er-ate!

We all have our jobs.
We all get a chance
to pass out papers
and to water the plants.

Have no doubt.

We help each other out.

We cooperate!

Cooperate!
Cooperate!

When we all work together,
  it's great.
It's great!

It's a long, long word,
but it must be heard.
Let's co-op-er-ate!

We move our chairs
to make more space.

Let's move our chairs
to another place.

They're so heavy,
but it'll be easy
when we cooperate!

One, two, three,
can you help me?

Four, five, six,
I'm in a fix!

I can't do it all alone,
not on my own!

Seven, eight,
let's cooperate!

Cooperate!

Cooperate!

When we all work together, it's great.

It's great!

It's a long, long word,
but it must be heard.
Let's co-op-er-ate!

# SONG LYRICS
## Let's Cooperate

Cooperate!
Cooperate!
When we all work together, it's great.
It's great!

It's a long, long word,
but it must be heard.
Let's co-op-er-ate!

When I play a game
and it's more than just me,
we all have fun
when it's two or three.

Here at school,
we play by the rules.
We cooperate!

Cooperate!
Cooperate!
When we all work together, it's great.
It's great!

It's a long, long word,
but it must be heard.
Let's co-op-er-ate!

We all have our jobs.
We all get a chance
to pass out papers
and to water the plants.

Have no doubt.
We help each other out.
We cooperate!

Cooperate!
Cooperate!
When we all work together, it's great.
It's great!

It's a long, long word,
but it must be heard.
Let's co-op-er-ate!

We move our chairs
to make more space.
Let's move our chairs
to another place.

They're so heavy,
but it'll be easy
when we cooperate!

One, two, three,
can you help me?

Four, five, six,
I'm in a fix!

I can't do it all alone,
not on my own!

Seven, eight,
let's cooperate!

Cooperate!
Cooperate!
When we all work together, it's great.
It's great!

It's a long, long word,
but it must be heard.
Let's co-op-er-ate!

# Let's Cooperate

**Indie Pop (Folk/World)**
**Musical Youth Productions**

**Verse 2**
We all have our jobs. We all get a chance
to pass out papers and to water the plants.
Have no doubt. We help each other out.
We cooperate! (Interlude x2)

**Verse 3**
We move our chairs to make more space.
Let's move our chairs to another place.
They're so heavy, but it'll be easy
when we cooperate! (No Interlude)

**Chorus** (Interlude x1)

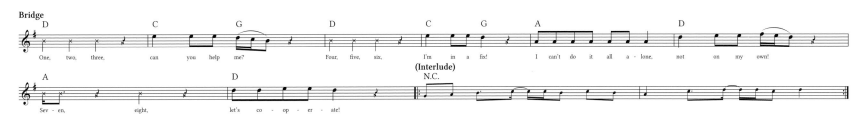

**Chorus** (To Coda)

# GUIDED READING ACTIVITIES

1.  How do you cooperate with your classmates at school? How about with your family at home? How do you cooperate with your friends?

2.  Imagine what life would be like if we didn't cooperate with each other. What things would be more difficult to do?

3.  Draw a picture of your favorite way to cooperate. It could be playing a game or a sport or helping someone.

## TO LEARN MORE

Cook, Julia. *Teamwork Isn't My Thing and I Don't Like to Share*. Boys Town, NE: Boys Town Press, 2012.

Gregory, Helen. *Teamwork*. Mankato, MN: Capstone Press, 2013.

McDonald, James. *An Operation of Cooperation*. Salem, OR: House of Lore, 2013.

Smith, Sian. *Manners at School*. Mankato, MN: Heinemann-Raintree, 2013.